People Around Town / Gente de mi ciudad

MEET THE FARMER/ CONOCE A LOS GRANJEROS

By Joyce Jeffries

Traducción al español: Eduardo Alamán

Gareth Stevens Publishing

Please visit our website, www.garethstevens.com. For a free color catalog of all our high-quality books, call toll free 1-800-542-2595 or fax 1-877-542-2596.

Library of Congress Cataloging-in-Publication Data

Jeffries, Joyce.
Meet the farmer = Conoce a los granjeros / by Joyce Jeffries.
p. cm. — (People around town = Gente de mi ciudad)
Parallel title: Conoce a los granjeros.
In English and Spanish.
Includes index.
ISBN 978-1-4339-9466-1 (library binding)
1. Farmers—Juvenile literature. 2. Occupations—Juvenile literature. I. Jeffries, Joyce. II. Title.
S519.J44 2013
630—dc23

First Edition

Published in 2014 by
Gareth Stevens Publishing
111 East 14th Street, Suite 349
New York, NY 10003

Editor: Ryan Nagelhout
Designer: Nicholas Domiano

Photo credits: Cover, p. 1 Alexander Raths/Shutterstock.com; p. 5 Stockbyte/Thinkstock.com; pp. 7, 9, 11, 13, 17, 19, 24 (tractor, Henhouse) iStockphoto/Thinkstock.com; p. 15 Joy Brown/Shutterstock.com; p. 21 Nancy Honey/Cultura/Getty Images; pp. 23, 24 (tilapia) Greg Vaughn/Perspectives/Getty Images.

Printed in the United States of America

CPSIA compliance information: Batch #CS13GS: For further information contact Gareth Stevens, New York, New York at 1-800-542-2595.

Contents

Contenido

Farmers feed
your family!

¡Los granjeros
alimentan a nuestras
familias!

They live off the land.

Viven de los frutos
de la tierra.

A big machine helps
them plant seeds.
This is called a tractor.

Una máquina grande
les ayuda a sembrar.
Este es un tractor.

They grow plants
like wheat.

Los granjeros cultivan
plantas como el trigo.

They take care
of animals.

Cuidan a los
animales.

Their cows and goats give us milk!

¡Sus vacas y cabras nos dan la leche!

Dogs are used
to herd sheep.

Los perros se usan
para reunir las ovejas.

Farmers raise horses. You can ride horses on a farm!

Los granjeros crían caballos. ¡Tú puedes montar a caballo en una granja!

Chickens get their own home. This is called a henhouse.

Las gallinas y los pollos tienen su propia casa.
Se llama gallinero.

Tilapia are raised on fish farms.

Algunos peces, como la tilapia, se crían en granjas.

Words to Know/ Palabras que debes saber

henhouse / (el) gallinero

tilapia / (la) tilapia

tractor / (el) tractor

Index / Índice